The Five Mile Press

LIVIN' THE PREDATOR LIFESTYLE
the Sparrows
No Kats
Robins
the Martins
Kats stay out

Too
sunny!

YOU AND
WHAT ARMY?

WORKING OUT
ISN'T WORKING OUT

TO EAT OR NOT TO EAT?

THAT'S A SILLY QUESTION!

SNACK ATTACK!

Z
CHIPS
SLEEP:
the Perfect Exercise

Garfield Green Tip:
Plant a tree.

OLDER & WIDER

JUNGLE

FEVER

I Spy a Blubber Brain!

JUST OBSERVING STUPID IN ITS NATURAL STATE.

The Anti-Diet Cat!

NEVER TRUST
A SMILING CAT

BORN TO EAT BIG
GARFI

PARTY POOPER

DO I LOOK LIKE I CARE?

MAD CAT

SLEEPY CAT

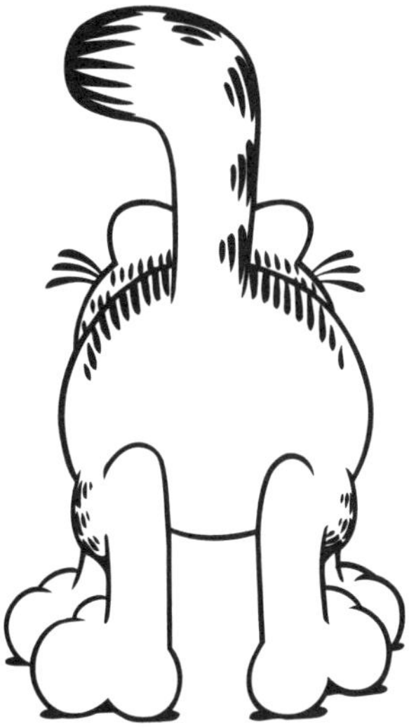

HAPPY CAT

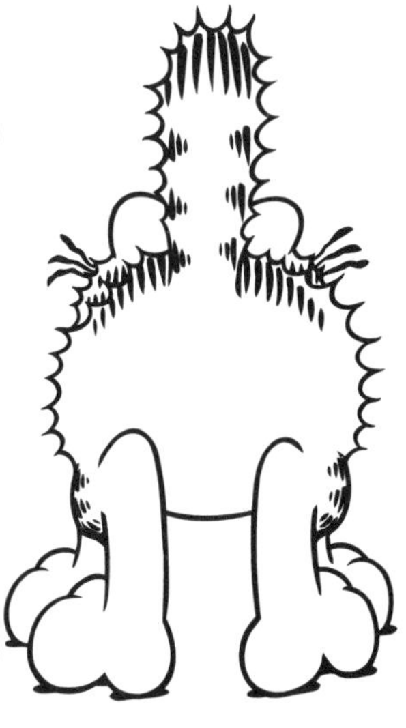

SCAREDY CAT

CAT MAKING A LEFT TURN

HUNGRY CAT

DON'T KNOW

DON'T CARE

Garfield
BEEFS UP!

CLEANING IS OVERRATED.
VHS
OLD YELLA
DVD
FORCE

NO DIETS!

COOK LIKE A DAREDEVI

BUT IT WAS ON SALE ...
SALE
SALE
DRESS Shoppe
Le Perfum

SHUT UP, I'M EATING

A Cookie a Day ...

HOLIDAY SEASON = FOOD
ODIE
POOKY
Santa

MINE

NO DIETS!
KISS the COOK

LIFE IS ~~a WALK IN THE PARK~~

Exhausting!

Don't Kiss the Chef

Forget humans

pets rule!

MAKE LUNCH, NOT LANDFILLS!

GRILL

POWER

SNACK TIME!

NO SHARING, NO CARING.

FORGET CIVILISATION

WALK THE PLANK!

I HATE SPIDERS!
I HATE WINDY DAYS
I HATE WAX DOUGHNUTS
SWOOSH
FWANG!
Z

ENOUGH COLOURING ... BRING ME LASAGNE